THIS BOOK BELONGS TO

....

DATE

....

A FAMILYLIFE BOOK

Thanksgiving

A TIME TO REMEMBER

Barbara Rainey

CROSSWAY BOOKS • WHEATON, ILLINOIS

THE LANDING OF THE PILGRIMS.

THANKSGIVING
Copyright © 2002 by Barbara Rainey
Published by Crossway Books
  a division of Good News Publishers
  1300 Crescent Street
  Wheaton, Illinois 60187

Second edition © 2003 by Barbara Rainey.

Cover and interior design: UDG | DesignWorks (www.udgdesignworks.com)
First printing 2002
Printed in Singapore

Scripture quotations are taken from the *New American Standard Bible*® Copyright © The Lockman Foundation 1960, 1962, 1963, 1968, 1971, 1972, 1973, 1975, 1977. Used by permission. (www.Lockman.org)

Library of Congress Cataloging-in-Publication Data
Rainey, Barbara.
  Thanksgiving : a time to remember / Barbara Rainey.
    p. cm.
  ISBN 1-58134-538-0 (HC : alk. paper)
1. Thanksgiving Day--History. I. Title.
  GT4975 .R35 2002
  394.2649--dc21
                                    2002009546

IM 14 13 12 11 10 09 08 07 06 05 04 03

15 14 13 12 11 10 9 8 7 6 5 4 3 2 1

THANKSGIVING CD
Produced by Keith Lynch and Allan Mesko
Piano arrangements: Allan Mesko
All other arrangements: Keith Lynch

Piano: Allan Mesko
Classical Guitar, MIDI Programming: Keith Lynch
Trumpet: Tom Richeson
Flute: Sarah Mesko
Percussion: Brian Brown
Upright Bass on Doxology: Jay Gentry
Doxology Vocal: Jani Quay
Assistant Engineers: Jonell Lynch, Ian Lynch

To My Family
both my children and my extended Peterson family:
Thanks for our wonderful Thanksgiving holidays.

And to the Families of America
May you grow in gratitude for our Christian heritage.

Table of Contents

Thanksgiving Joy

Welcome Home

Summer vacations, late night sunsets, and a more relaxed schedule are behind us. School has resumed with its ballgames and homework deadlines. The nesting instincts of a mom rise to the surface as she again thinks about nurturing her family with comforting chilies and soups. She's thinking about the status of everyone's winter coats and hats and gloves, making sure those in her care are protected. It's time for the stability of a routine, the security of the familiar, and the safety of a family. It's time to come home.

Welcome home.

"We gather together to ask the Lord's blessings." So begins a wonderful hymn often sung at Thanksgiving. Although most Americans' lives don't center around a literal harvest anymore, many of us do gather together every year on the fourth Thursday of November to enjoy family and partake of the abundance of this land.

Increasingly I've heard people say that Thanksgiving is their favorite holiday. Is that surprising? Though it's a holiday sandwiched between the increasingly popular Halloween and the overwhelmingly merchandised Christmas, Thanksgiving remains the holiday of "coming home." It's a holiday of rest—in stark contrast to the frenzy of obligations and spending that threaten to destroy the essence of Christmas.

Our national observance of Thanksgiving is unique. It is both distinctly Christian and exclusively American, a holiday for celebrating faith, family, and freedom.

Having majored in history in college, I've been concerned for years that "we the people" don't know and understand what Abraham Lincoln referred to when he began his famous Gettysburg address with the statement: "Fourscore and seven years ago, our fathers brought forth upon this continent a new nation, conceived in liberty. . . ." I was determined that my children would hear the stories of the courageous men, women, and children who lived honorably and, through faith in God, made enormous sacrifices to secure freedom for us all. I wanted them to understand God's sovereignty at work in the lives of our forefathers and His providential direction of their circumstances. For the Rainey family Thanksgiving was not going to be just eating, hours of TV, football, naps, and leftover turkey sandwiches—followed by a stress-filled Friday of frantic Christmas shopping at the mall.

With my husband's help I initiated some new traditions into our Thanksgiving Day. The two more important ones are the reading of stories about the Pilgrims' journey of faith from England to the shores of Cape Cod and the recording and sharing of our family's personal blessings. As believers in Christ, we have so much to be thankful for, and, as Americans, God has abundantly blessed our nation.

This book contains a remarkable story of faith. Our forefathers were ordinary men and women, but they possessed an extraordinary faith. Their courage will inspire us, their perseverance will challenge us, and their faith will be an example to us. May we get to know them and follow in their footsteps.

This story should be read aloud, which can be done in a variety of ways, depending on your family's size, children's ages, and circumstances. For the last ten or more years we have read the entire story on Thanksgiving morning. Our younger children sometimes got restless and bored with some of the story, but they learned that the story came first and then the food. Some years to keep the children involved and interested, I had the older ones read different parts of the story.

You will notice that the book is printed in two different sizes of type. The larger-type sections contain the essence of the Pilgrim story and the parts that would be most interesting to younger children. Reading only the larger-print sections will take about thirty minutes. Each larger-print section is written to flow from one section to another even though you skip the smaller-print portions of the story. As a second option, the entire Pilgrim story, beginning on page 17, can be read straight through all sections, both large and smaller type, in about fifty minutes. A third approach would be to read one of the six sections each day leading up to Thanksgiving.

TWO BOOKS IN
ONE TO READ ALOUD
ON
THANKSGIVING DAY

*Read only the large type
sections for young children.*
Or
*Read both the large type
and small type sections together
for families with older
children, teens, and
adults.*

In addition, sidebars contain extra information on various topics such as Massasoit, the Indian leader who was so instrumental in the Pilgrims' survival; the history of our Thanksgiving holiday; and others about feasting, gratitude, and more. These are not designed to be read aloud as a part of the Thanksgiving story, but can be read at another time to supplement your family's understanding of the Pilgrim experience and to provide application for our lives today.

Also included is a CD of Thanksgiving instrumental music designed for you to play on Thanksgiving Day and all week long. Our hope is that this music will call your heart to gratitude as you listen to familiar hymns and choruses of worship, praise, and thanksgiving.

In summary, you decide what will work best for your family. My advice is to keep it as simple as possible. If your children are young, read only a few paragraphs that you think they will especially enjoy. As they get older, you can add more of the story each year. The point is to build a tradition of remembering the past, recognizing God's hand in our history, and expressing gratitude to Him for His goodness. Reading this story has become a wonderful tradition for our family, and I hope it will be for your family too.

May God bless you and your family.

—BARBARA RAINEY

Robert W. Weir. 1803-1889

The Pilgrim Story

The Mayflower at Sea, 1620

Small Beginnings

The *Mayflower,* a small wooden ship with billowing sails, was the vessel God used to bring a group of Christian believers to an unseen land far over the Atlantic. These Christian men and women, called Pilgrims (people who journey to a destination usually because of their religious beliefs), believed that God was leading them to establish a new community where they could worship freely.

As Americans, we celebrate Thanksgiving every year because of the profound faith and uncommon courage of these English men and women. They had no idea how God was going to use them to begin a new nation. They only knew God wanted them to go.

So in September of 1620, after enduring many delays and difficulties, these Pilgrims finally said their last good-byes, boarded the *Mayflower,* and set sail for the New World.

The roots of our Thanksgiving heritage are entwined with the history of England, growing deep into the rolling green hills of the English countryside. Nestled in those hills was a little village named Austerfield. And in that village in 1590 a child named William Bradford was born.

William's childhood was unhappy. While still a boy, he was orphaned, his father dying when he was a baby, his mother when he was seven. He was placed in the home of two uncles in Austerfield. Not long after his mother died, William suffered a prolonged illness that left him unable to work in the fields. As a result, he was allowed to be educated, and he learned to read the Bible on his own.

As a teenager, he walked every week to a nearby village called Scrooby to learn more of the Christian faith and to worship God secretly in a personal and pure way with a small group of like-minded believers. Increasingly, William grew dissatisfied with the state-sponsored religion of the Church of England. Its worship seemed stale and cold compared to what he experienced with the believers in Scrooby.

Like many people of his time, William concluded that there wasn't much hope for spiritual life to return to the state church. Those who felt this way were called "Separatists," individuals willing to risk the consequences of "separating" from the official church. There was another group of people in the English church who became known as "Puritans." The Puritans also disagreed with the state church, but they wanted to stay in the church and try to purify or change it from within.

The authorities in the Church of England felt threatened by both of these growing movements toward religious freedom. They especially feared the Separatists who were forming their own churches. So the governing House of Bishops sent spies and informers to many of these secret congregations, including the one at Scrooby. Many Separatist church leaders and some Puritans were fined, pressured, persecuted, arrested, or thrown in prison. Some were even executed with the approval of Queen Elizabeth I and later King James I in hopes of squelching these rebellious believers. After years of mounting stress caused by this harassment and persecution, many families in the Separatist church—including William who was not yet twenty—left their English homeland for exile in Leyden, Holland.

The Separatists enjoyed their new religious freedom in Holland, but life again became increasingly difficult for them. In England many of them had been landowners. In Holland, because they were foreigners, the men had to take whatever work was available.

> *Though a portrait of William Bradford does not exist, his journals and letters clearly reveal the heart of this man who walked with God.*
>
> *"…what does the Lord require of you, but to do justice, to love mercy, and to walk humbly with your God."*
>
> MICAH 6:8

William Bradford became a weaver, usually working twelve- to fourteen-hour days, six days a week. The Separatists did not complain, however, because the ability to worship God as they saw fit was supremely important. They lived out the message of Hebrews 12:28: "Since we receive a kingdom which cannot be shaken, let us show gratitude, by which we may offer to God an acceptable service with reverence and awe."

After nearly a decade on Dutch soil, a number of members of the church of Leyden began to explore the possibility of moving across the sea to the "new world" of America. Many of them once again wanted to own their own land, and because England was such a powerful country in Europe and in the world, they feared that the English might pressure the Dutch government to clamp down on the "rebel church." The Separatists also worried about the effect of a rather morally "loose" Dutch society on their own young people.

But the challenges of life in the wild territory across the Atlantic were sobering. Other groups had settled in America with disastrous results. The Jamestown colony in Virginia was a recent example: Of 1,200 settlers who had arrived in Jamestown in 1619, only 200 were still alive in 1620.

The congregation in Leyden debated the decision. Staying in Holland meant greater safety in a civilized land. Settling in America probably guaranteed religious liberty, but the physical risks were enormous, and the financial cost of a voyage would be high. America was an uncivilized frontier with a vicious climate in some regions. Would the farming techniques they knew work in this new land? What strange diseases might await them there? Perhaps worst of all, the land was filled with "savages" about whom frightening stories were told by those who had sailed back from the New World.

In spite of this sobering outlook, the Leyden church chose to believe that God would grant them success if they sent a settling party to America. William Bradford later wrote, "They had a great hope and inward zeal of laying a good foundation, for the propagating and advancing of the kingdom of Christ in those remote parts of the world; yea though they should be but even as stepping stones unto others." If God blessed their efforts, then many others—including their pastor, John Robinson—probably would join them on the other side of the Atlantic Ocean.

William Bradford was one of those who decided to embark on the adventure. During the exile in Holland, he had met and married a young woman named Dorothy May. The couple later had a son named John, who was particularly precious to his mother. Because of the anticipated hardships awaiting the Separatists in America, as well as the rigors of the ocean voyage, some decided to leave family members behind in Holland.

They hoped that in the near future all could be reunited in the new land. This was true of the Bradfords who sadly chose to leave five-year-old John in the care of others.

After all the discussion and agonizing decision-making—and before departing from Holland—the church spent a day in fasting and prayer for the journey ahead. Then they gathered for a special service and to hear a sermon from their pastor. He chose as his Scripture text Ezra 8:21: "Then I proclaimed a fast…that we might humble ourselves before our God to seek from Him a safe journey for us, our little ones, and all our possessions."

After Pastor Robinson had encouraged and prayed for the group of Pilgrims, the entire Separatist congregation had a feast and sang psalms. Edward Winslow, one of the church leaders who would be making the voyage, wrote of the evening: "We refreshed ourselves, after our tears, with the singing of Psalms…and indeed it was the sweetest melody that ever mine ears have heard."

Following God's Call

The Pilgrim band of approximately forty-six people first had to sail from Holland to England on a ship named the *Speedwell*. After sad farewells, on July 22, 1620, the small ship headed across the English Channel to the seaport of Southhampton. The *Speedwell* docked at a slip next to a ship painted brown and gold. It was the *Mayflower*. Already on board this ship were Captain Jones, his crew, and sixty to seventy volunteers who had been recruited in England to give the new colony a larger population. Some of these volunteers desired religious freedom, but most were more interested in finding success and fortune in the new land. Also on board were some servants hired to help the Pilgrims from Leyden. One of the hired helpers was Captain Miles Standish, an ex-soldier who would play an important role in the months ahead.

Both the smaller *Speedwell* and the *Mayflower* sailed from Southhampton on August 5, 1620. This was late in the summer to launch such a voyage. Even with a normal ocean crossing and no bad weather, the ships would not arrive until October—quite late to start building a settlement from the ground up.

The first days of the journey hinted at difficulties to come. The winds were unfavorable, and the ships could not make it out of the English Channel. The passengers, bounced to and fro by the rough waters, became seasick. Then the *Speedwell* began to leak. Seawater seeped through the hull and filled the belly of the ship. Both ships were forced to return to land, this time to the port of Dartmouth.

After a week repairs were completed on the *Speedwell,* and both ships sailed west. After traveling about 300 miles into the Atlantic, the *Speedwell* again developed leaks. With great disappointment to everyone, the ships returned a second time to yet another port—Plymouth.

More days of work and testing by shipbuilders passed before the *Speedwell* was labeled unseaworthy. The smaller *Speedwell* had been purchased by the colony to remain in America and be a means of transporting supplies, goods for sale, and passengers back and forth to Europe. But because the ship couldn't be repaired, the Pilgrim leaders were forced to sell it. This necessitated another decision. Since there wasn't enough room on the *Mayflower* for the combined passengers of both ships, twenty volunteers would have to stay behind. Apparently the choice was not too difficult since by now they had spent much of the last month on board ship and had experienced considerable seasickness. The volunteers came forward. William Bradford commented, "And thus like Gideon's army, this small number was divided, as if the Lord by this work of his providence thought these few too many for the great work he had to do."

When the *Mayflower* finally left England, on the 6th of September, crowded on board were 102 passengers, including thirty-three children. Most of the Pilgrims on the ship were in their twenties and thirties. Surprisingly, at least fifteen passengers were over forty, including William and Mary Brewster, who were both in their fifties.

Because of the delays, the passengers and crew had already used much of the food and drink set aside for the voyage. This meant supplies intended for use after landing in America would be needed for the sea journey. The food was terrible—brine-soaked beef, pork, and fish and stale, hard biscuits, which often were full of insects. The rats living on board helped themselves to the same food supplies.

The rooms for passengers were crowded and mainly below deck. Conditions were miserable: cramped quarters, seasick people vomiting into pails—if they were able to find one in time, no sanitary toilets; the hatches were sealed off because of constant storms, and so the passengers were unable to get fresh air. A foul mixture of odors grew in such an environment.

Another problem was the attitude of the seamen sailing the *Mayflower*. These men did not like "landlubbers," particularly religious ones, calling the Pilgrims "psalm-singing puke-stockings" and worse! The sailors ridiculed their passengers for taking time each morning to recite or sing psalms and pray. One young sailor was especially nasty, cursing the ones who were sick and telling them he looked forward to throwing them overboard if they died on the voyage.

About two weeks out to sea, this same sailor unexpectedly developed a raging fever. Within just one day he died of an unknown sickness, raving and cursing as he breathed his last. His shrouded body was buried at sea. This sobered the other seamen, a superstitious group even in normal circumstances. They wondered if their fellow crewman had died because of his treatment of the humble and God-fearing Pilgrims. Not wanting to risk a similar fate, the more superstitious sailors no longer ridiculed their passengers.

The *Mayflower* was nearly halfway across the Atlantic when it met a ferocious storm. The wind wailed

The children who rode the *Mayflower* to New England, as well as those born in the new land, endured the same hardships their parents did: They were hungry and cold and wet. They picked up on their parents' apprehensions about the Indians. If the children were old enough, they too worked in the fields, fished for food, and gathered wood.

But they were still children. And since children almost everywhere go to school to learn to read and write, what did the "Plimoth" (the word was first spelled this way) children do? William Bradford wrote in 1624 that though they could not have a common school because there was no teacher, they certainly wanted to start a school. In the meantime, Bradford reported, many parents taught their children as best they could on their own.

These boys and girls may have been the children of Pilgrims, but they were not perfect. As Proverbs 22:15 says, "Foolishness is bound up in the heart of a child." The proverb applied to Pilgrim children as well.

On December 5, after living in the new land less than a month, one mischievous boy nearly caused a disaster. While his father, John, was absent, Francis Billington went into his cabin (the family was still living on the *Mayflower*) and started playing with his father's guns. In *Mourt's Relation* we read that he picked one up and "shot her off in the cabin; there being a little barrel of powder half full, scattered in and about the cabin, the fire being within four feet of the bed between the decks, and many flints and iron things about the cabin, and many people about the fire." It appears that Francis, who was a teenager and should have known better, actually shot the gun. The spark from the shot caused a small fire, but the barrel of gunpowder nearby did not explode. The account ends with these words: "by God's mercy, no harm done."

The following summer another boy wandered into the woods and got lost. A search party was formed, and the group departed

on June 11 with Squanto and Tokamahamon, another Indian, as guides. The group sailed across the bay toward what is now Barnstable, Massachusetts. That first night darkness fell before they could put into shore, and so they spent the night on the water.

In the morning Indians came to the shore to catch lobsters. Squanto and Tokamahamon were sent to assure them that the Pilgrims meant no harm and were

just searching for a lost boy. The Indians replied that the boy was well, but he was with another tribe at Nauset.

That evening the searchers took the boat to Nauset and sent Squanto to speak to the *sachem* (chief) of this tribe, with whom they had not yet made peace. Again *Mourt's Relation* provides the details: "After sunset, Aspinet, their chief, came with a great train, and brought the boy with him, one bearing him through the water. He had not less than a hundred with him, the half whereof came to the shallop side unarmed with him; the other stood aloof with their bows and arrows. There he delivered us the boy, behung with beads, and made peace with us."

Stories of girls could not be found in these early accounts. I think they probably were watched more closely and were given tasks at home such as baby-sitting siblings and learning to sew and cook for the family. Certainly, they did not have as much freedom to wander the woods and streams on errands for family meals.

Surviving these several hundred years is a sampler made by Loara Standish, daughter of Captain Miles Standish. A sampler was a piece of linen cloth on which a young girl would practice her sewing stitches. It usually finished with a rhyme and the girl's

name and the date. Here is what Loara Standish stitched on her sampler:

Loara Standish is my name.
Lorde guide my hart that
I may doe thy will also
My hands with such
Convenient skill as may
Conduce virtue void of
Shame and I will give
The glory to thy name.

Records do exist though of the names of some of the girls. Those in the Separatist church and the Puritans who were still in England had a custom of choosing names for their children that fit an occasion, had a special meaning, or were found in the Bible. Here are the names (with original spellings) of the girls: Ellen More, Mary Allerton, Remember Allerton, Pricila Mullins, Constanta Hopkins, Damaris Hopkins, Humility Coper, Eelizabeth Tillie, Mary Chilton, Desire Minter.

The Pilgrim boys included some with unusual names that must have had a special meaning for their parents that we don't understand today: Bartholomew Allerton, Francis Billington, John Billington, Love Brewster, Wrasling Brewster, John Cooke, Giles Hopkins, John Crakston, Samuell Eaton, Samuell Fuller, John Hooke,

Oceanus Hopkins, William Latham, Jasper More, Richard More, Joseph Mullins, Joseph Rogers, Henery Samson, Resolved White, and four unnamed boys.

Some of the children on the *Mayflower* did not have biological parents with them. Undoubtedly they had been orphaned and later adopted by caring families. The three More children were listed as siblings, but all three lived with separate families. John Hooke was brought as a "servant boy," and Henery Samson and Humility Coper lived with their cousins Edward and Ann Tillie.

We know that the children survived the first winter better than the adults. Some children died in the following years, but others lived long lives and had many children of their own. Eelizabeth Tillie married one of the servant boys and had ten children. Love Brewster had four children, as did both Remember and Mary Allerton. Pricila Mullins married John Alden and had eleven children. Constanta Hopkins had twelve, Henery Samson had seven, and one of the Billington sons had eight.

The Pilgrim children were normal boys and girls who, when they became adults, continued the legacy their parents began. And because of them, a nation was born.

at fifty miles per hour, and waves towered fifty feet or higher. The waves' vicious pounding opened cracks in the ship's wooden hull. Icy cold seawater soaked the sailors and leaked into the passenger quarters below deck. The ship rolled and tossed from side to side with the terrified Pilgrims hanging on to anything solid, crying out to God to deliver them.

The storm raged for days and became so intense that even the blasphemous sailors prayed. The Pilgrims continued to pray and sing psalms—their voices barely heard above the thundering waves and howling wind.

Without warning one of the huge crossbeams supporting the main deck suddenly cracked due to the constant stress of the high winds. Now the sailors were as worried as the passengers. But as always the Pilgrims took their concerns and fears to God, asking Him to deliver them and provide a way of escape. And He did. Their spiritual leader, William Brewster, remembered the large iron jack screw the Pilgrims had brought for lifting heavy beams when they would begin their building construction. Similar to the screw on his printing press, the jack screw was located in the cargo hold and carried to the 'tween deck, where the sailors used it to crank up the beam to its original position. The Pilgrims gave God the praise.

One man, a servant of John Carver named John Howland, became frantic after being cooped up so long during the long storm. Though the worst of the storm was over, the main deck was still no place for passengers who were not used to rough seas. He disobeyed both the captain's and his master's orders and went up on deck for some fresh air. The waves were still huge and sprayed frigid water over the sides. Suddenly when the ship heeled over without warning, John fell overboard. As the young man slammed into the surface of the icy water and went under, he instinctively reached up with his arms, grasping for anything to hold on to. A rope was trailing over the side of the ship, and by God's amazing grace it was there when John reached out.

The average temperature in the north Atlantic in November is 10.2° C. or about 40-50° F.

A person can live in the north Atlantic in November for only about four minutes. No one knows exactly how long John was in that cold, salty water before the sailors were able to haul him on deck. His skin was blue, and he had nearly drowned, but he did survive. There's no record that he ever disobeyed an order again.

Another young man, a servant by the name of William Butten, became an example to all the other passengers on the importance of obeying the captain. It appears that William refused to follow the captain's and the ship's doctor's orders to drink a spoonful of lemon juice daily. He became sick and died, the only passenger to die on the voyage. His body was quickly buried at sea. The Pilgrims, especially the children, took notice.

In the midst of tragic events and hardships on the long voyage, the Pilgrims also knew times of rejoicing. A moment of joy came when one of the mothers gave birth in the smelly, crowded cabin to a baby boy. His proud father appropriately named the lad Oceanus.

But after ten weeks at sea many passengers were falling ill and complaining of fever, chills, and swollen limbs. The situation was grave, and there was still no sign of land.

The weather, however, had finally improved so that passengers could go on deck for exercise and fresh air. Captain Miles Standish, in charge of security and military readiness for the colony, took this opportunity to drill the men on the basics of weaponry and tactics.

On November 9 several children squealed with delight when they saw a seagull dive above the ship. Not long afterward a sailor cried, "La-a-nd, ho!"

After sixty-five days at sea from Plymouth (a total of ninety-seven days from the first launch at Southhampton), the Pilgrims caught a glimpse of their destination, the new land where
God would be worshiped freely and—in time—where freedom would flourish.
Shouting for joy and falling to their knees to pray, they celebrated by reading
Psalm 100:

Shout joyfully to the Lord, all the earth.

Serve the Lord with gladness;

Come before Him with joyful singing.

Know that the Lord Himself is God;

It is He who has made us, and not

we ourselves;

We are His people and the sheep of His pasture.

Enter His gates with thanksgiving,

And His courts with praise.

Give thanks to Him; bless His name.

For the Lord is good;

His lovingkindness is everlasting,

And His faithfulness to all generations.

NEW ENGLAND

The most remarqueable parts thus named.
by the high and mighty Prince CHARLES,
Prince of great Britaine

Jean Leon Gerome Ferris, 1863-1930

Mayflower Compact, 1620

Sustained by God's Grace

With land clearly in sight—brownish bluffs and treetops on the horizon—the *Mayflower* sailed slowly up the coastline, staying out to sea far enough to avoid the treacherous shoals and rocks nearer shore. The passengers eagerly eyed what they could see of what is now the northern tip of Cape Cod. Because of the difficult seas they had encountered, the Pilgrims had made their landfall about sixty miles north of their intended destination at the mouth of the Hudson River. The leaders on board wondered what to do. Should they sail back to the south where their charter with the Virginia Company would be in effect, or should they find a suitable harbor and settle here? Had God in His providence led them to this spot?

After much debate and prayer, they decided to stay and build their settlement in "New England." When all of the passengers heard of this decision, confusion and some dissension broke out. The bonded servants on board argued that this plan changed the terms of their work agreement. Fear rose that these men would declare their independence and leave the Pilgrims with a depleted labor supply. Something needed to be done to bring about unity.

For an entire day, November 10, 1620, a discussion went on in the main cabin of the *Mayflower.* As the ship worked its way around the tip of the Cape, searching for a coastal inlet to enter and drop anchor, the debate continued. Finally several of the leaders drafted an agreement, the Mayflower Compact, which was to become one of the more important documents in American history. The major points of the agreement were explained to the passengers, and all adult males were asked to sign the compact before the ship dropped anchor. According to the book *The Light and the Glory,* by Peter Marshall and David Manuel, "…it marked the first time in recorded history that free and equal men had voluntarily covenanted together to create their own new civil government."

The key clauses contained these words:

Having undertaken for the Glory of God and advancement of the Christian Faith and Honour of our King and Country, a voyage to plant the First Colony in the Northern Parts of Virginia, do by these presents solemnly and mutually in the presence of God and of one another, Covenant and Combine ourselves together into a Civil Body Politic, for our better ordering and preservation and furtherance of the ends aforesaid…

With the compact signed, a hedge against revolt was in place. Next the last bit of business was conducted—the election of John Carver as governor of the colony for a one-year term.

By this time the *Mayflower* had sailed beyond the end of the cape and turned into a bay. The Pilgrims saw more clearly the landscape of sand hills and thickets of short piney woods. At 10 A.M. Captain Jones ordered the anchor dropped. It was Saturday morning, November 11, 1620. William Bradford wrote later of this moment: "I cannot but…stand half amazed at this poor people's present condition;… Being thus past the vast ocean, and a sea of troubles…they had now no friends to welcome them nor inns to entertain or refresh their weather-beaten bodies;…What could now sustain them but the Spirit of God and His grace?"

Bradford also noted the custom of the Pilgrims to honor God and give thanks in all things: "…they fell upon their knees and blessed the God of heaven who had brought them over the vast and furious ocean, and delivered them from all the perils and miseries thereof, again to set their feet on the firm and stable earth, their proper element."

A party of men armed with muskets and axes was sent ashore to explore the land and secure firewood, since they had none left on the ship. The group returned in the afternoon with juniper logs, which soon were burning in cooking fires on board. The Pilgrims enjoyed their first hot meal in weeks.

Although everyone was eager to go ashore and begin construction of the settlement, because the next day was Sunday, all work stopped and the Sabbath was observed as usual with prayer, meditation, singing of psalms, and a sermon by William Brewster. It was a custom they observed faithfully every week in all circumstances in obedience to the fourth commandment.

In the days that followed, several expeditions were made to explore the area to seek the best location for a settlement. Winter weather now made this effort miserable. The Pilgrim men and the sailors who chose to go along endured freezing rain and rough waves as they rowed across the bay. One day they met Indians on shore without incident, but the next day were attacked. Though many arrows were shot at the men, and musket fire was returned, no one was injured. Again the Pilgrims gave thanks to God for His protection and deliverance. They called the place First Encounter, as it is still called to this day.

In spite of these difficulties, the men were successful, having slowly made their way by land and by sea around the interior of the Cape. They eventually found an ideal spot on the mainland

The people who belonged to the Separatist church believed the Bible literally. They knew God's message to His people well. In the Old Testament, God related to His people, the Israelites, by means of covenants, which is an agreement between God and the people He chose. In the New Testament, God still relates to His people by means of a covenant. However, the New Testament covenant is called the New Covenant because it is totally different from the old, being instituted by the life, sacrificial death, and resurrection of Jesus Christ. The Old Covenant was meant for a nation, while the New Covenant is meant for a kingdom of people from every tribe, nation, and language who have believed on Jesus Christ for salvation.

The Separatists journeyed to this new land to proclaim by their lives this message of redemption, the New Covenant and the light of Christ. They knew God's promises—His Word. They knew He would keep His covenant Word to them as they went forward by faith. So they obediently gave thanks in all things, and boldly they prayed for all their needs.

This covenant that God established with His people became their model for the Mayflower Compact as well as for the peace treaty they established with Massasoit and his people. They knew a God who keeps His word, and therefore they were faithful to keep their word, their promises to one another and to others. This covenant is a model that still endures today.

But the essence of God's covenant relationship with His people is that it is personal. To be in covenant with God is an exchange of lives. I give Christ my life, and in return He gives me His. It's certainly not a fair trade because we are not equals. But because God is love and His whole focus on this world is its redemption, He delights in having our lives. Then He can do what He does best—begin to redeem our lives and our mistakes and use them for great good. I'd rather have Jesus' power than mine, His love than mine, His attitudes than mine, His perspective than mine, His peace than mine. I'd rather trust Him than myself.

Are you in covenant with God? Have you given Him your life as the Pilgrims did? It's a huge decision but a simple transaction. Give Jesus Christ your life by faith and invite Him to live inside you. That's the exchange—His life for yours. Once you've made that exchange, you are in covenant with God, and you belong to the New Covenant kingdom of believers from every tribe and nation and language.

William Bradford

that had fertile soil, four spring-fed creeks, and a large section of ground already cleared and ready for planting. The men rejoiced at their discovery.

During these explorations, many colonists back on board the *Mayflower* became gravely ill, and a few died, including William Bradford's young wife, Dorothy. There was little time for mourning and sadness. Their desperate condition demanded that they all work, especially the men, to establish the colony.

It wasn't until December 11, a month after they had first dropped anchor, that a landing was made at what was to become the permanent settlement. Plans had been made to first build a meetinghouse and then nineteen family dwellings, the unmarried men having been assigned to live with families. These buildings were to be simple one-room frame houses, about eighteen by fourteen feet in size, with a fireplace and a sleeping loft. There was no glass for the windows, and the roofs were made of thatch, which the settlers had used in England. Construction finally began in late December.

A disheartening setback occurred in mid-January when the thatched roof of the newly completed meetinghouse caught on fire. Fortunately the settlers put out the flames before the whole building burned.

By the end of January several family dwellings were partially built, but most of the Pilgrims were still living in temporary quarters in the meetinghouse and on the *Mayflower*. Captain Jones had graciously agreed to delay his return with the *Mayflower* to England. He knew that the settlers needed its protection.

Perhaps the Pilgrims had felt that the worst was over when they finally set foot on solid ground again. But their relief was only momentary. Though they were hard workers, they could not build their dwellings quickly enough. And they could only endure the harsh winter weather without ill effect for so long.

As the weeks went by, the weather grew worse. In the coldest stretch of winter, after many had suffered long with head colds, a flu-like illness swept through the colony. This disease, called the "general sickness," had made much of the community desperately ill. Coughing and gasping for breath, most of the settlers were unable to leave their beds. Few were spared. William Bradford, Governor Carver, and other leaders fell sick too. During the worst of the epidemic, on any given day only six or seven out of the hundred colonists might be strong enough to help tend the sick.

The Pilgrims began to die in alarming numbers—often two or three each day. The men strong enough to work carried the bodies out for burial at night. This was a tactic to hide the worsening situation in the colony from any Indians who might be spying from the nearby woods.

One of the men who remained healthy and tirelessly helped the others was the military leader, Captain Miles Standish. Even after his own wife, Rose, died on January 21, Standish continued to serve the others faithfully.

The epidemic also struck the sailors on board the *Mayflower*. Those Pilgrims still on their feet ministered to the sick sailors too, prompting one of the sailors—a man who had ridiculed and cursed the God-fearing passengers during the sea crossing—to say, "You, I now see, show your love like Christians indeed one to another, but we let one another lie and die like dogs."

February brought the worst of the weather and the sickness. Freezing rains pounded the crude dwellings, stripping much of the clay from the cracks between boards and allowing the wailing, cold wind to penetrate the houses. Both the sick and healthy struggled to stay warm. Seventeen persons died during the month.

Indians were sighted on several occasions. Since the intentions of the native people were unknown, the colonists were very fearful. Under the leadership of Captain Standish, the men who were not too ill practiced military drills and shared guard duty at night.

Hope began to grow again as temperatures rose slightly in early March. A few families began preparations for planting their crops. But the most memorable event in March, perhaps of the whole winter, was the arrival on March 16 of a single nearly naked Indian brave. Unlike other Indians who ran away when confronted, this man strode boldly to the door of the meetinghouse and, to the surprise of all, cried out, "Welcome," in English!

Stunned by his boldness and use of English, yet still wary of his intentions, the Pilgrims hesitantly invited him in and offered him a plate of food and some brandy. The Indian ate and drank enthusiastically.

After his meal, the Indian informed his hosts that he knew English food and customs through contacts with English fishermen. The settlers learned that his name was Samoset. (He was a chief of the Algonquins, and his home tribe was farther up the coast to the north in what is now Maine.) He said that the Indians who had inhabited this area were called the Patuxets. They were a large Indian tribe who had murdered every white man who had ever landed in their territory. But four years before the Pilgrims arrived, the tribe suffered a mysterious plague, and everyone had died.

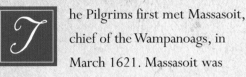 he Pilgrims first met Massasoit, chief of the Wampanoags, in March 1621. Massasoit was described by Emmanuel Altham, who arrived as a visitor in the colony in 1623, as "a very proper man and very courageous." Altham wrote that his appearance was like all his men, "all naked but only a black wolf skin upon his shoulder" and with a loin cloth and a string of beads around his waist. Another early writer also told of the Indians wearing leather shoes and breeches, which was their winter attire.

Early in that first important meeting with Massasoit, the Pilgrim leaders made a peace agreement with him and his people, knowing how necessary it was to their survival to have these neighbors as allies and friends. There were only six agreements, which stated basically that they would treat each other honorably, not steal from one another, and not cause harm to one another. They also agreed to come to the aid of one another if either was attacked in war.

Massasoit was agreeable to these terms since he was a peace-loving man and was a kind leader of his people.

God was clearly at work in the lives of the Pilgrims and in their circumstances. He was also interested in the Indians, wanting them to know of Him as a personal God who could be believed and trusted. In March of 1623, word came to the colony that their friend Massasoit was sick and about to die. Governor Bradford sent Edward Winslow, another man, and their interpreter, Hobbamock, along with some medicines to offer what help they could. After two days of travel, they arrived and were told the chief was already dead. Hobbamock was much distressed and said grieving to Mr. Winslow, "I should never see his like among the Indians. He was no liar; he was not bloody and cruel like others; he was easy to be reconciled towards such as offended him; he governed his men better with few strokes than others did with many; he was truly loving and oft times restrained the malice of others."

Winslow was concerned over their loss and what it might mean for the colony, but he decided to "leave the event to God in His mercy," continuing on to Massasoit's lodge another five or six miles away. Upon arriving, they found that the chief was not dead but very close to death. Winslow spoke to him and asked if he could give him some of the medicine he had brought. Though his sight was gone, and he hadn't swallowed anything in over two days, Massasoit submitted to Winslow's treatment. Winslow writes, "Within half an hour this wrought a great alteration in him in the eyes of all who beheld him. Presently his sight began to come to him, which gave him and us good encouragement."

For the next two days, Winslow ministered to him, making him broth and helping him rest, which before his arrival had been impossible because his people had gathered around shouting incantations, "making a hellish noise." In the end Massasoit fully recovered, and Winslow wrote, "We with admiration blessed God for giving His blessing to such raw and ignorant means, making no doubt of his recovery, himself and all of them acknowledging us the instruments of his preservation. Never did I see a man brought so low, recover in that measure in so short a time."

Massasoit said, "Now I see the English are my friends and love me; and whilst I live, I will never forget this kindness they have showed me."

And he didn't. Before the Pilgrim men left to return to Plymouth, Massasoit revealed to them that the Massachusetts Indians and seven other neighboring tribes had plotted together to kill all the English, both the Plymouth colony and the new one farther north. He explained that they had come and asked him to join in the plan while he was sick, but he refused. He then gave advice about how to deal with this very real threat. The men returned to Plymouth and informed the governor, who, with the advice of the other leaders, intervened and stopped the threatened annihilation.

Once again God provided for His people and protected them. They were serious about obeying His Word and dealing with the Indians in a loving, respectful way, and God honored their choices.

Neighboring tribes were so surprised by the tribe's misfortune and total demise that they avoided the area, fearing they too would be killed by the plague. As a result no one lived on the land, and no one owned it. It was another example of God's remarkable provision for the Pilgrims.

Samoset went on to explain about the other Indian tribes in the surrounding area. The nearest Indians lived about fifty miles south of Plymouth. They were the Wampanoags, which means "People of the Dawn." They were a friendly tribe headed by their chief, or *sachem,* Massasoit. With Samoset's help the Pilgrims planned to make contact with braves from the Wampanoags to trade for animal skins.

Near the end of March, with the weather improving and the worst of the influenza outbreak over, the surviving Pilgrims assessed their winter losses. Several entire families had perished in the epidemic; fifteen of nineteen women were dead; in only four couples had both spouses survived. The children had fared best. Of ten girls, nine survived, and only eight of twenty-three boys died. Nearly half of those who had arrived on the *Mayflower* now lay in the shallow graves dug on a windswept hill beside the sea.

The South part of New-England, as it is Planted this yeare, 1634.

William Brewster

God's Perfect Provision

With the days lengthening and the temperatures warming, the Pilgrims turned their attention to planting the crops desperately needed if they were to survive a second winter in America. But they were interrupted by the reappearance of their new friend, Samoset, who arrived at the settlement with five Indians. Though the Pilgrims didn't know it at the time, one of these Indians would play perhaps the largest role in the survival of "New England." Bradford wrote of him that he was "a special instrument sent of God for their good, beyond their expectation." His name was Tisquantum, or "Squanto" for short. Squanto also spoke English, because years earlier he had been captured by a treacherous sea captain and taken to Europe as a slave. Since Squanto had been away when the plague wiped out his tribe, he was the lone surviving Patuxet from the Plymouth area. He had been back in his native land for only six months.

Because Squanto's English was quite good, he was asked to take the role of lead translator when the Pilgrims met Massasoit. Within a week a meeting was arranged where gifts were exchanged, a pipe smoked, and an agreement reached that guaranteed peace between the Pilgrims and this Indian tribe. This peace pact would last for fifty years! As the days passed, both Indians and Pilgrims met frequently in the nearby woods without incident. The Pilgrims rested more easily.

Squanto stayed on in Plymouth and "adopted" these families as his own, "never leaving them until he died," Bradford wrote. It was clear they needed his help and his invaluable practical knowledge. He showed the

WHERE DID FEASTING ORIGINATE?

easts of Thanksgiving didn't begin in America with presidential proclamations. They didn't begin with the grateful Pilgrims in Plymouth. Neither did they originate with the Native Americans' harvest celebrations. The true source of feasting as a celebration of gratitude is God Himself.

In the Old Testament, God initiated a number of yearly feasts for His people the Israelites. These were not optional events, but were written into the Law that God gave to Moses on Mt. Sinai. God knew better than His children the importance of setting aside time to reflect on His abundant provision for them. When we focus on God's goodness and His character, we are not only grateful, but we are motivated to believe Him for more. Our faith grows as we remember His past intervention in our lives.

The first feast God instituted was the Feast of Unleavened Bread, which commemorated the Israelites' deliverance from bondage in Egypt. It was a time to remember the miraculous way God had set them free and then led them out of Egypt and into the Promised Land.

The Feast of Harvest, the second celebration in the calendar year, was for the purpose of dedicating the first fruits of the new crops. This event was followed by the Feast of Ingathering, which occurred at the end of the harvest season. This third occasion of feasting was set aside to celebrate God's abundant harvest provision.

The joyful mood of thanksgiving in all of the Old Testament feasts is represented well in this psalm:

Oh give thanks to the LORD,
call upon His name;
Make known His deeds among the peoples.
Sing to Him, sing praises to Him;
Speak of all His wonders.
Remember His wonders which He has done,
His marvels and the judgments
uttered by His mouth.
—Psalm 105:1-2, 5

Pilgrims how to catch eels and fish at the river to use as fertilizer for their planting of corn. This crop would save their lives in the winter to come. He taught them how to plant pumpkins and tap the maple trees for syrup. And for their economic benefit he introduced them to the trade of trapping beaver for their pelts. This skill too would be important for their future survival.

In early April Captain Jones decided it was time to sail the *Mayflower* home to England. With the spring sunshine restoring the health of the colonists, he felt it was now safe to leave. Even after all the hardships and many deaths, every Pilgrim in the colony elected to stay in Plymouth rather than return to the homeland.

With increasing hours of daylight and recovered strength, everyone in the colony soon enjoyed a pleasing weekly rhythm of work and worship. Six long days the Pilgrims tilled, hunted, fished, mended, built, cooked, and washed. The only break in routine each week was on Sunday when the group faithfully observed the Sabbath. On this day ordinary work clothes were exchanged for more colorful attire. Unlike the somberly clothed Puritans, who in the years to come would settle farther to the north, the Plymouth colonists wore brightly colored dresses, suits, and hats. In garments of blue, red, green, violet, and yellow the congregation sang, prayed, and listened to a rousing sermon by their elder, William Brewster.

Springtime turned the thoughts of some away from the grief of lost husbands and wives to new love. The first remarriage occurred in May between two of the widowed—Edward Winslow and Susanna White. The wedding reception gave everyone an opportunity to laugh, sing madrigals, and enjoy special food and drinks.

Another potential romance almost turned tragic. Two young men, both named Edward, fell in love with a beautiful fifteen-year-old girl named Constance. The rivalry became so intense that the two suitors decided a duel was the only way to decide who should win the girl. The two Edwards met on the beach and began to fight with daggers and swords. Both drew blood, but their shouts alerted other colonists. Several men came running and separated the two before either was killed.

Apparently Constance was unimpressed. She chose not to marry either Ed.

In August during some conflict among Indian tribes, the friend of the Pilgrims—Squanto—was taken hostage and threatened with death. Under the leadership of Miles Standish, an armed detail left Plymouth to rescue him. In the middle of the night the Pilgrims burst into the village where Squanto was a hostage. After a brief fight, in which several Indian braves suffered sword wounds, Squanto was rescued unharmed. This aggressive military action made such an impression on all of the area tribes that within days new peace treaties were agreed to by all parties.

The First Thanksgiving, 1621

Jean Leon Gerome Ferris, 1863-19

God's People Give Thanks

By October 1621 the corn planted that spring was ready for harvest. The fields yielded a large crop that would keep the colony from starvation in the coming winter. Their hearts were full of gratitude for their renewed health, for the abundant harvest, and for the peace they enjoyed with the Indians.

William Bradford, who at only thirty years of age had been elected leader of the colony after the death of John Carver that summer, was thankful for the harvest. As the new governor, he declared that Plymouth should hold a thanksgiving festival and invite the settlement's Indian friends as special guests. A date was set, and an invitation delivered to Chief Massasoit.

To make sure there was adequate food, the Pilgrim men went hunting and fishing. In just a day enough wild turkeys, eels, geese, lobster, partridge, and shellfish were gathered to guarantee a great feast. But when Massasoit arrived with ninety hungry braves—all smeared with ceremonial bear grease—the Pilgrims became worried. How could they feed that many people? And if they used too much of their precious stock-piled corn, would they have an adequate food supply to survive the winter?

Fortunately the Indians along the Atlantic coast also were accustomed to celebrating the harvest—with what they called the Green Corn Dance; they thought the Pilgrim festival must be the white man's version of this observance. So when Massasoit and his men arrived at Plymouth, they too went to the woods and seashore to gather food. Soon five deer and more fish and seafood were presented for roasting. The Pilgrims breathed a sigh of relief and began preparing the meal.

When it was time to eat, the menu was impressive: venison, goose, lobster, eel, oysters, clam chowder, parsnips, turnips, cucumbers, onions, carrots, cabbage, beets, radishes, and dried fruit that included gooseberries, strawberries, cherries, and plums. Some of the fruit was cooked inside dough to make a crude pie. The newly harvested corn was ground and served in the form of ashcakes or hoecakes, a thin slice of bread baked in a fire on the blade of a hoe. A special treat was supplied by the Indians. They placed corn on hot coals, and the kernels blew into white puffs—popcorn! The Indians dribbled maple syrup over the white snack and made popcorn balls. The beverage was a fresh wine made by the Pilgrims from the summer's fruit crop.

But before they began to eat, their spiritual leader offered a prayer to the God who had so clearly and miraculously led them to this place. Though they had suffered much, their experience was remarkably better than others who had attempted to colonize on the American shores. Plymouth had lost 50 percent of its numbers, but Jamestown in Virginia had lost 90 percent. The Plymouth settlers had successfully built a little community and grown crops to provide for themselves, while other colonies were totally dependent for supplies on the arrival of ships from England. Yes, God had blessed them abundantly, and they sincerely offered Him their thanks and praise.

The feasting continued over a three-day period, during which both Indians and Pilgrims participated in games and exhibitions of shooting skill with bows and arrows and guns. The Pilgrim boys joined the races and wrestling matches of the Indians, and in turn the Indians learned how to play stoolball—a game resembling croquet played with a ball and wickets.

At night the Indians slept in nearby fields. The relationship between the settlers and Indians was now so solid and peaceful that the Pilgrims no longer posted guards.

When the fun and feasting ended, both Indians and colonists agreed they wanted to have a similar feast the following year.

Grumbling or Gratitude?

oes it ever seem surprising to you that God made the Israelites wander in the wilderness for forty years because they grumbled? My kids may have spent thirty minutes in their rooms for griping, but forty years? What a severe discipline! Ouch, it seems harsh.

God clearly is not pleased with grumbling. It doesn't make Him happy to hear His children complain constantly. Sound like any children you know?

Being grateful is a choice. It's not a feeling dependent on our circumstances, as we clearly see in the Pilgrims' lives. They believed that God was in control—"Providence," they called it. They responded to the circumstances of their lives with a perspective that said, "God has allowed this for our good."

John Piper has written in his book *A Godward Life*: "Remembering our dependence on past mercies kindles gratitude. Gratitude is past-oriented dependence; faith is future-oriented dependence. Both forms of dependence are humble, self-forgetting and God-exalting. If we do not believe that we are deeply dependent on God for all we have or hope to have, then the very spring of gratitude and faith runs dry."

Gratitude is what we express when we take time every Thanksgiving Day to remember God's past mercies and provisions and then pause to thank Him for them.

The stories of those who have gone before us inspire our faith. When we consider those great saints listed in the "Hall of Faith" in Hebrews 11 or our Pilgrim forefathers or those men and women we know in recent times who have modeled great dependence on God, our faith is stretched and increased. Their example of placing all hope in Jesus Christ encourages us to do the same.

Hebrews 11:1 says, "Now faith is the assurance of things hoped for, the conviction of things not seen." Those who sailed on the *Mayflower* knew their Bible well. They were convinced that God existed and could only be pleased through faith (Hebrews 11:6).

Someone has said, "Faith is a firm conviction, a personal surrender, and a conduct inspired by your surrender." The Pilgrims were totally surrendered to God, and they believed that He was leading them to the New World. So they went, confident that He would guide and provide.

The Bible is full of verses on giving thanks. Our problem in America is not that we don't know we are to be thankful, but often we choose to complain instead. The Psalms contain a number of verses that call thanksgiving a sacrifice:

Offer to God a sacrifice of thanksgiving. (Psalm 50:14)

He who offers a sacrifice of thanksgiving honors Me. (Psalm 50:23)

Let them also offer sacrifices of thanksgiving. (Psalm 107:22)

To You I shall offer a sacrifice of thanksgiving, and call upon the name of the LORD. (Psalm 116:17)

Why is it a sacrifice to give thanks to the Lord? Because being thankful forces us to take our eyes off ourselves and put them on the Lord. Giving up our self-focus is the kind of denial that pleases God.

As a nation, we have inherited a remarkable gift in our freedom to worship, but we have strayed far from our roots and heritage. We must return to the faith of our fathers. Developing a heart of gratitude is the beginning step in growing a stronger faith. Remember what God has done and believe that He will take care of us in the future.

Giving Thanks in All Things

In November, a ship from England, the *Fortune,* arrived unexpectedly and delivered thirty-five new colonists, which nearly doubled their numbers. Though they were delighted to see these fresh faces, some of which belonged to family members, the existing residents were sobered to realize that the new recruits had come without extra food, clothing, or other provisions. Soon after the newcomers were assigned to families in the colony, the leaders met to plan for their survival. Governor Bradford and William Brewster reached the difficult decision: Everyone would go on half rations through the winter.

The abundant harvest of corn they had so recently stored for that second winter of 1621-1622 was now not nearly enough. They began that winter cautiously with everyone getting their half ration of corn, hopeful that the men could find enough game and fish to see them through. Supplies dwindled quickly. Legend has it that at one point the food stores were so low that everyone was forced to a daily ration of only five kernels of corn. It's amazing to think that anyone could survive on so little food; yet no one died of starvation.

Once again at the height of their need, God provided deliverance. Another ship sailed into their harbor, and though it did not have food, the captain did have trading goods that he offered in exchange for beaver pelts. With the trading goods, the Pilgrims bartered with the Indians for more corn. The extra corn enabled them to survive the second winter, although they were all considerably thinner.

When the spring of 1622 finally arrived, the colony was much weakened by hunger and sickness, and the famine was not over. The weary Pilgrims went to the fields to plant their common crops, but their enthusiasm was greatly reduced. However, they continued on with the life that God had given them. They had many dealings with their Indian friends, continued exploring the land, and obtained what sustenance they could by fishing, hunting, and bartering with the Indians. Edward Winslow described their sad condition that spring, saying that the bay and creeks were full of fish, but their seines and netting were torn and rotten. He wrote that were it not for shellfish of different kinds that could be taken by hand, they would have perished.

Another colony was begun to the north, and other ships arrived in Cape Cod Bay several times that year, usually bringing colonists without supplies of any kind. Neither Bradford's journal nor the writings of other Pilgrims record a thanksgiving celebration in that second harvest season. Bradford did write, "the welcome time of harvest approached, but it arose but to a little. So it well appeared that famine must still ensue the next year also."

Again God saw them through the winter of 1622-23 by means of another ship, which brought trading goods they could use to barter for corn with the Indians.

Planting time was soon upon them in April of 1623. Their needs were desperate. The Pilgrims realized they had to plant double the previous year's crop to sustain them in the winter to come. This year it was decided they would seed a common cornfield for the whole colony, and then each family would be given a parcel of land to plant for its own use. Everyone was enthusiastic, for they were eager to grow as much as possible to avoid another "starving time." William Bradford observed, "This had very good success; for it made all hands very industrious, so as much more corn was planted than otherwise would have been. The women now went willingly to the field and took their little ones with them to help set corn."

Soon after the plantings, however, the weather turned dry. As the weeks of drought went by, the Pilgrims watched their precious summer crops wither and slowly die. The Indians said they had never seen a dry spell like it. After twelve weeks the Pilgrims realized they would face certain starvation in the coming winter if it did not rain soon. The colonists were losing hope. They wondered if God, who had always gone before them, was against them. They began to pray. William Bradford asked everyone to participate in a day of fasting and prayer to ask the Lord for rain.

All the Pilgrims felt a deep sense of humility before God, and they sincerely sought His mercy. Edward Winslow described what happened:

> But, O the mercy of our God, who was as ready to hear, as we were to ask! For though in the morning, when we assembled together, the heavens were as clear and the drought as like to continue as it ever was, yet...before our departure [from the day of prayer and fasting], the weather was overcast, the clouds gathered on all sides. On the next morning distilled such soft, sweet and moderate showers of rain, continuing some fourteen days. . . such was the bounty and goodness of our God!

Bradford wrote, "...It came, without either wind or thunder, or any violence, and by degrees in that abundance as that the earth was thoroughly wet and soaked therewith. Which did so apparently revive and quicken the decayed corn and other fruits, as was wonderful to see and made the Indians astonished to behold...."

If the Pilgrims were amazed at God's answer to their prayers and His great deliverance, imagine how wide-eyed with wonder the Indians were. They had no knowledge of the God of the Pilgrims, a personal benevolent God who cared about His people. God was displaying His wonders.

Winslow concluded his description of this miraculous event with his thoughts on the Indian's response:

> ...all of them admired the goodness of our God towards us, that wrought so great a change in so short a time, showing the difference between their conjuration [rain dances] and our invocation on the name of God for rain, theirs being mixed with such storms and tempests, as sometimes, instead of doing them good, it layeth the corn flat on the ground, to their prejudice, but ours in so gentle and seasonable a manner, as they never observed the like. Praise the Lord, great things He hath done!

The crops were saved.

Another answer to prayer came about two weeks later. The ship *Anne,* which was carrying many family members and friends to join the

Did you know there once was a day set aside to remember and celebrate the lives of our nations founders? It was December 22 commemorating the day in late December when the Pilgrims finally were able to go ashore and begin building their meeting house. Founders' Day, or Forefathers' Day as it was sometimes called, was celebrated briefly in the 1760s.

In 1777 the first national day of thanksgiving was declared by the Continental Congress following the providential victory at Saratoga over the British. In 1789 the newly formed U.S. Congress passed a resolution requesting "a day of public Thanksgiving and prayer to be observed by acknowledging with grateful hearts the many signal favors of Almighty God, especially by affording them an opportunity peaceably to establish a Constitution of government for their safety and happiness." President George Washington signed that proclamation and declared Thursday, November 26, 1789, as the first national Thanksgiving Day.

As the years passed, the holiday was celebrated sporadically. State governors would sometimes issue proclamations and sometimes not, often setting different dates from year to year.

A magazine editor named Sarah Josepha Hale helped organize a movement to make Thanksgiving a national holiday. Every year from 1846 to 1863, Mrs. Hale printed an editorial in her magazine urging the government to establish this holiday. The date Mrs. Hale desired was July fourth! It was a logical choice, but as the Thanksgiving momentum increased, others proposed a November date. Finally, in 1863, in the midst of the Civil War, President Abraham Lincoln set aside the last Thursday of November as a day of national "Thanksgiving and praise to our beneficent Father who dwelleth in the Heavens."

Lincoln declared another Thanksgiving Day the following year, as did his successor, Andrew Johnson. Other presidents followed the new tradition annually with the holiday landing in December for a few years.

The date for Thanksgiving was again changed briefly in 1939 to the third Thursday in November, but a public uproar of opposition caused the U.S. Congress to establish the fourth Thursday as the holiday date. President Franklin D. Roosevelt signed a bill on November 26, 1941, that finally established the fourth Thursday of November as our national Thanksgiving Day.

colony, had been reported lost at sea, but now it arrived safely at Plymouth harbor. The newcomers, however, were shocked and dismayed at the condition of their friends and relatives. Bradford wrote that it was no wonder the newcomers were surprised. The Pilgrims were thin and gaunt, wearing ragged clothes, "some little better than half naked." The only food they could offer in welcome was a lobster or piece of fish, with no bread and nothing else but a cup of spring water. Bradford concluded by saying, "But God gave them health and strength in good measure and showed them by experience the truth of the word in Deuteronomy 8:3: That man lives not by bread alone, but by every word that proceeds out of the mouth of the Lord."

The daily ration of bread was one-quarter pound per person.

That harvest season was an abundant one. There was even a surplus to trade with the Indians for what they needed that winter. They had much to celebrate. Another day of Thanksgiving was planned this year, probably in August or September. The Indians were again invited with their chief, Massasoit.

It was a season of gratitude. They were grateful for the rain and the harvest. They were grateful for the safe arrival of their family members and friends. They were grateful for the marriage of their wise Governor Bradford to Alice Southworth, who had also arrived on the *Anne.*

Lastly and most importantly, they celebrated with grateful hearts God's goodness to them. Edward Winslow wrote that "having these many signs of God's favor and acceptance, we thought it would be a great ingratitude if secretly we should content ourselves with private thanksgiving for that which by private prayer could not be obtained [referring to the day of prayer and fasting earlier that summer]. And therefore another solemn day was set apart and appointed for that end; wherein we returned glory, honor, and praise, with all thankfulness to our God who dealt so graciously with us."

As they expressed their gratitude and thanksgiving to God, they remembered the famine they had so recently experienced. No one would soon forget the meager rations they had lived on for nearly two years.

Though they didn't soon forget, we have.

Nearly four hundred years later, we who are the beneficiaries of their sacrifice pause at the end of the harvest season to celebrate a day of Thanksgiving. There are many lessons we can learn from this story, but they all come back to faith. The Pilgrims sailed to America because of their faith. They wrote the Mayflower Compact based on God's Word and signed it by faith. They persevered in the harsh climate because of their faith. They befriended the Native Americans because of their faith. Their uncompromising belief in God and His Word became the cornerstone of the colony and in turn of the new nation.

It is doubtful that the Thanksgiving celebration in 1623 began with five kernels of corn on each plate as tradition tells us. The recent famine was too fresh in their memories to need a visual reminder. It is, however, a tradition that should be continued in our generation. William Bradford once wrote these words that should stir our hearts to greater levels of thankfulness for all we possess and enjoy: "We have noted these things so that you might see their worth and not negligently lose what your fathers have obtained with so much hardship."

May we Americans remember every year what a rich legacy we have been given so we might express gratitude to God and "not negligently lose what [our] fathers have obtained with so much hardship."

Lincoln's 1863 Thanksgiving Proclamation

Taken from the collection of Lincoln's papers in the Library of America series, Vol II, pp. 520-521.

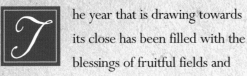

The year that is drawing towards its close has been filled with the blessings of fruitful fields and healthful skies. To these bounties, which are so constantly enjoyed that we are prone to forget the source from which they come, others have been added, which are of so extraordinary a nature, that they cannot fail to penetrate and soften even the heart which is habitually insensible to the ever watchful providence of Almighty God. In the midst of a civil war of unequalled magnitude and severity, which has sometimes seemed to foreign States to invite and to provoke their aggression, peace has been preserved with all nations, order has been maintained, the laws have been respected and obeyed, and harmony has prevailed everywhere except in the theatre of military conflict; while that theatre has been greatly contracted by the advancing armies and navies of the Union. Needful diversions of wealth and of strength from the fields of peaceful industry to the national defence have not arrested the plough, the shuttle, or the ship; the axe had enlarged the borders of our settlements, and the mines, as well of iron and coal as of the precious metals, have yielded even more abundantly than heretofore. Population has steadily increased, notwithstanding the waste that has been made in the camp, the siege and the battle-field; and the country, rejoicing in the consciousness of augmented strength and vigor, is permitted to expect continuance of years with large increase of freedom.

No human counsel hath devised nor hath any mortal hand worked out these great things. They are the gracious gifts of the Most High God, who, while dealing with us in anger for our sins, hath nevertheless remembered mercy. It has seemed to me fit and proper that they should be solemnly, reverently and gratefully acknowledged as with one heart and voice by the whole American People. I do therefore invite my fellow citizens in every part of the United States, and also those who are at sea and those who are sojourning in foreign lands, to set apart and observe the last Thursday of November next, as a day of Thanksgiving and Praise to our beneficent Father who dwelleth in the Heavens. And I recommend to them that while offering up the ascriptions justly due to Him for such singular deliverances and blessings, they do also, with humble penitence for our national perverseness and disobedience, commend to his tender care all those who have become widows, orphans, mourners or sufferers in the lamentable civil strife in which we are unavoidably engaged, and fervently implore the interposition of the Almighty Hand to heal the wounds of the nation and to restore it as soon as may be consistent with the Divine purposes to the full enjoyment of peace, harmony, tranquillity and Union.

—Abraham Lincoln

1. For God's
   succeeded
   of a Godly

2. For God's p
   for one j
   today.

3. For fam
   examples
   our ow

4. For H
   couples

5. For
   God's
   harder

1. Ashley can come home
2. family
3. MO + Mayo
4. that I got
5. for a gree

Laura

1. I'm thankful for mom, because she is so awso...
   to teach deborah and I.
2. Dad, Because he teaches the class so well...
   all my friends have learned a lot.
3. I'm thankful that I did not break my
   right arm and Left arm at the same time.
4. For the Godsees for being so genours to the children
   around them.
5. I am thankful for my older sibleing who
   come just to be with the rest of us.

Lest Anyone Forget

What a remarkable story of faith and courage. I am inspired and motivated by the lives of these men and women every time I read about their choice to believe God in all circumstances. Reading of God's faithfulness to them encourages me to believe God for more in my own life.

After you've read the Pilgrim story with your family, some time on Thanksgiving Day have everyone present share five things he or she is grateful for during the past year. We do this at our home on Thanksgiving morning. Everyone's place at the table is set with five kernels of corn and a card and a pen.

The kernels of corn are a reminder to us of the meager rations the Pilgrims lived on during their second and third years in Plymouth. The corn is a visual remembrance of the sacrifice they made for us. We then pass a small basket around the table, and as everyone puts a kernel of corn in the basket, each shares one item from his or her list of Thanksgiving blessings. The basket goes around the table five times. We then hold hands and offer a prayer of gratitude to God for His abundant blessings and for the ways we have seen Him at work in our lives.

Years ago, when we first started having our children record

things for which they were thankful, I had no intention of keeping all their little scribblings and childish sentences. So they wrote and colored on notebook paper or whatever I could find that was handy. My point was to teach them to reflect and be grateful.

But I did keep a few of their lists, and now I wish I'd kept them all. The earliest ones I can find are from the year our youngest daughter Laura was two and a half. I don't have everyone's for that year, only Laura's scribbles and what I wrote that she said, and her older sister Rebecca's, printed carefully on her second grade manuscript paper.

We have a big gap between those pages from 1987 and the next collection of Thanksgiving cards in 1993. That was the year I finally began to make it a point to have everyone record a list of five blessings after we read the Pilgrim story on Thanksgiving Day. We've been faithful to our tradition ever since. We've been through a lot in those years: junior high, sending kids to college, learning our son

has a form of muscular dystrophy, sending another son to Estonia for a year, homeschooling, accidents, speeding tickets, and now marriages and grandchildren.

Our family's sharing on Thanksgiving morning has become one of our highlights of the year. Reviewing what God has done in our lives is healthy, and it is biblical. Psalm 105:5 tells us to "Remember His wonders which He has done, His marvels and the judgments uttered by His mouth." By contrast, Psalm 106 tells what happens when we, as God's people, don't remember what He has done. It says of Israel: "They did not remember Thine abundant kindnesses.…They forgot God their Savior.… They did not believe in His word, but grumbled in their tents."

May we resolve to be a grateful people in this nation, and may we not forget what God has done and what those who have gone before have sacrificed for us.

God bless your family as you share this story together. Celebrate the "Faith of Our Fathers," and may Thanksgiving become your favorite holiday as you focus on faith, family, and, freedom.

OUR FAMILY REMEMBERS

God's Blessings

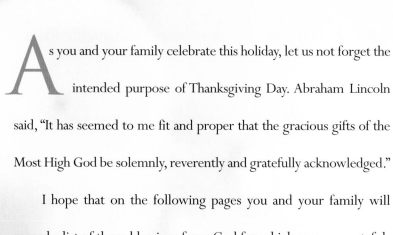

As you and your family celebrate this holiday, let us not forget the intended purpose of Thanksgiving Day. Abraham Lincoln said, "It has seemed to me fit and proper that the gracious gifts of the Most High God be solemnly, reverently and gratefully acknowledged."

I hope that on the following pages you and your family will record a list of those blessings from God for which you are grateful. In our family, each individual makes a list of five things for which he or she wants to give thanks. You may want to make a collective list. But take the time to record God's abundant favor to you and yours, pausing during the day to pray prayers of thanksgiving. And may you do this year after year after year. In time you will have a wonderful collection of "remembrances" of God's great goodness. Isaiah 12:4-5 says, *"Give thanks to the LORD, call on His name. Make known His deeds among the peoples; make them remember that His name is exalted.' . . . Let this be known throughout the earth."*

God's Blessings

Therefore, since we receive a kingdom which cannot be shaken, let us show gratitude,
by which we may offer to God an acceptable service with reverence and awe.
—HEBREWS 12:28

In everything give thanks;
for this is God's will for you in Christ Jesus.
—1 Thessalonians 5:18

Let the peace of Christ rule in your hearts, to which indeed you were called in one body;
and be thankful. . . . singing with thankfulness in your hearts to God. . . . giving thanks through Him to God the Father.

—COLOSSIANS 3:15-17

Devote yourselves to prayer,
keeping alert in it with an attitude of thanksgiving.
—Colossians 4:2

*...always giving thanks for all things in
the name of our Lord Jesus Christ to God, even the Father.*

—EPHESIANS 5:20

...and there must be no filthiness and silly talk, or coarse jesting,
which are not fitting, but rather giving of thanks.

—Ephesians 5:4

It is the living who give thanks to Thee, as I do today;
A father tells his sons about Thy faithfulness.

—ISAIAH 38:19

O LORD, Thou art my God; I will exalt Thee, I will give thanks to Thy name;
for Thou hast worked wonders, plans formed long ago, with perfect faithfulness.
—ISAIAH 25:1

"Give thanks to the LORD, call on His name. Make known His deeds among the peoples; make them remember that His name is exalted."...Let this be known throughout the earth.

—ISAIAH 12:4-5

Surely the righteous will give thanks to Thy name;
the upright will dwell in Thy presence.

—Psalm 140:13

I will give Thee thanks with all my heart; I will sing praises to Thee...
and give thanks to Thy name for Thy lovingkindness and Thy truth.

—PSALM 138:1-2

Give thanks to the LORD, for He is good;
For His lovingkindness is everlasting.
—PSALM 136:1

Oh, give thanks to the LORD, call upon His name;
Make known His deeds among the peoples.

—PSALM 105:1

He who offers a sacrifice of thanksgiving honors Me;
And to him who orders his way aright I shall show the salvation of God.

—Psalm 50:23

_____   _____

_____   _____

_____   _____

_____   _____

_____   _____

_____   _____

_____   _____

_____   _____

_____   _____

_____   _____

As you therefore have received Christ Jesus the Lord, so walk in Him,
having been firmly rooted and now being built up in Him and established in your faith,
just as you were instructed, and overflowing with gratitude.
—COLOSSIANS 2:6-7

I thank my God in all my remembrance of you.

—PHILIPPIANS 1:3

_____   _____

_____   _____

_____   _____

_____   _____

_____   _____

_____   _____

_____   _____

_____   _____

_____   _____

_____   _____

Sources

Bradford, William. *Bradford's History "of Plimoth Plantation."* Boston: Wright & Potter, 1901.

Bradford, William. *Of Plymouth Plantation 1620-1647.* Ed. Samuel Eliot Morison. New York: Alfred A. Knopf, 1952.

Demos, John. *A Little Commonwealth.* New York: Oxford University Press, 1970.

Ezell, John S., Fite, Gilbert C., and Frantz, Joe B., eds. *Readings in American History*, Vol. 1, 3rd ed. Boston: Houghton Mifflin Company, 1964.

Fleming, Thomas J. *One Small Candle.* New York: W. W. Norton, 1964.

Heath, Dwight B., ed. *Mourt's Relation, A Journal of the Pilgrims at Plymouth.* Bedford, Mass.: Applewood Books, 1963.

James, Jr., Sydney V. *Three Visitors to Early Plymouth.* Bedford, Mass.: Applewood Books, 1963.

Marshall, Peter and Manuel, David. *The Light and the Glory.* Tarrytown, N.Y.: Fleming H. Revell Company, 1977.

Matthews, Albert. "The Term Pilgrim Fathers and Early Celebrations of Forefathers' Day." Massachusetts Historical Society, 1914.

Penner, Lucille Recht. *The Thanksgiving Book.* New York: Hastings House Publishers, 1986.

Schmidt, Gary D. *William Bradford: Plymouth's Faithful Pilgrim.* Grand Rapids: Eerdmans Publishing Co., 1999.

Sechrist, Elizabeth Hough and Woolsey, Janette. *It's Time for Thanksgiving.* Philadelphia: Macrae Smith, 1957.

Winslow, Edward. *Good Newes from New England.* Bedford, Mass.: Applewood Books.

A PRONUNCIATION KEY FOR THE INDIAN NAMES:

Massasoit, Mass'-a-soyt

Wampanoags, Wamp'-a-nawgs

Hobbamock, Hobb'-a-mock

Patuxet, Pah-tux'-et

FOR MORE INFORMATION ON FAMILY RESOURCES, GO TO WWW.FAMILYLIFE.COM

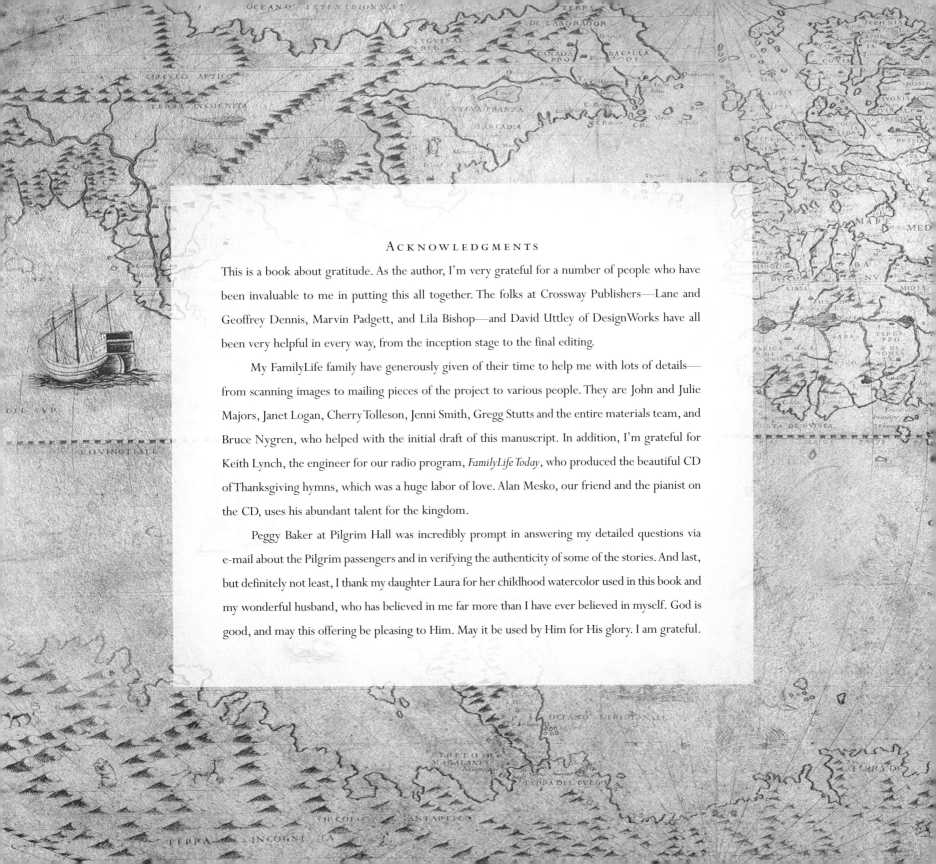

ACKNOWLEDGMENTS

This is a book about gratitude. As the author, I'm very grateful for a number of people who have been invaluable to me in putting this all together. The folks at Crossway Publishers—Lane and Geoffrey Dennis, Marvin Padgett, and Lila Bishop—and David Uttley of DesignWorks have all been very helpful in every way, from the inception stage to the final editing.

My FamilyLife family have generously given of their time to help me with lots of details—from scanning images to mailing pieces of the project to various people. They are John and Julie Majors, Janet Logan, Cherry Tolleson, Jenni Smith, Gregg Stutts and the entire materials team, and Bruce Nygren, who helped with the initial draft of this manuscript. In addition, I'm grateful for Keith Lynch, the engineer for our radio program, *FamilyLife Today*, who produced the beautiful CD of Thanksgiving hymns, which was a huge labor of love. Alan Mesko, our friend and the pianist on the CD, uses his abundant talent for the kingdom.

Peggy Baker at Pilgrim Hall was incredibly prompt in answering my detailed questions via e-mail about the Pilgrim passengers and in verifying the authenticity of some of the stories. And last, but definitely not least, I thank my daughter Laura for her childhood watercolor used in this book and my wonderful husband, who has believed in me far more than I have ever believed in myself. God is good, and may this offering be pleasing to Him. May it be used by Him for His glory. I am grateful.